CHRISTIANITY E✝PLORED

ENGLISH MADE EASY EDITION

Authentic

10 09 08 07 06 05 04   7 6 5 4 3 2 1

First published in 2004 by Authentic Media
9 Holdom Avenue, Bletchley, Milton Keynes, MK1 1QR, UK
and PO Box 1047, Waynesboro, GA 30830-2047, USA
www.authenticmedia.co.uk

BRITISH LIBRARY CATALOGUING IN PUBLICATION DATA
A catalogue record for this book is available from the British Library

ISBN 1-85078-581-3

Designed by Diane Bainbridge
Illustrations by Alex Webb-Peploe
Print Management by Adare Carwin

CHRISTIANITY EXPLORED

ENGLISH MADE EASY EDITION

STUDY GUIDE
FOR LEADERS

Section 1 – Training Notes

Section 2 – Study Guide

Welcome to the English Made Easy Edition of *Christianity Explored*.

This eight-week course of Bible study and discussion aims to introduce people to Jesus Christ through Mark's Gospel, in an environment where they are free to ask any questions they like.

The studies are written in simple English and are ideal for international students or those for whom English is a second language.

What makes this course – and the Christian gospel – distinctive is its insistence on God's remarkable grace: the clear teaching that although we human beings are rotten to the core, we are loved. Loved with an outrageous, daring, incomprehensible love and, what's more, loved by the One whose love we have treated as if it were unworthy of us.

It should be no easier for leaders to relate Jesus' teaching on sin, judgement, wrath and hell than it is for a course participant to hear it. But, if we are prepared to trust in the Holy Spirit's power to open blind eyes, these uncomfortable truths pave the way for a faithful life driven by God's abiding and abounding grace.

This book is divided into two sections: the first will train you to use the course, and the second will be your guide each week as you actually run the course.

If you do decide to run *Christianity Explored*, please let us know when and where your course is running. E-mail eme@christianityexplored.com or write to the General Manager, Christianity Explored, All Souls Church, Langham Place, London W1B 3DA, United Kingdom.

SECTION 1
TRAINING NOTES

This section will prepare you to lead participants through the course.

Session 1

Introduction

As we can see from his letter to the Romans, the apostle Paul was convinced that he could take the same gospel message to anyone: the Jewish theologians in first-century Jerusalem, the intellectual elite of imperial Rome and the pagans of Spain. But why? What made him such a confident evangelist?

Paul was not *self*-confident. He did not rely on his education, his intelligence or his eloquence. He did not depend on a thorough training in other world-views. Instead, his confidence was in the gospel itself. He said: 'I am not ashamed of the gospel.' And in Romans 1:16 we find out why:

> ## 'BECAUSE IT IS THE POWER OF GOD FOR THE SALVATION OF EVERYONE WHO BELIEVES'

The gospel is God's power to save anyone. It addresses every person, in every culture, in every nation.

It is universally relevant.

The reason the gospel is powerful to save is in verse 17:

> ## 'FOR IN THE GOSPEL A RIGHTEOUSNESS FROM GOD IS REVEALED, A RIGHTEOUSNESS THAT IS BY FAITH'

The gospel tells us that God will make righteous *anyone* who puts their trust in Christ.

It is universally accessible.

The reason the gospel is necessary is in verse 18:

'THE WRATH OF GOD IS BEING REVEALED FROM HEAVEN'

The gospel presents us with the only way we can be saved from God's wrath.

It is universally urgent.

Session 2

Crossing Cultures

There may be participants from a number of different cultures attending your course. With this in mind, it is important to be aware of some specific issues.

THE IMPORTANCE OF RELATIONSHIPS

In many cultures, an individual's identity is rooted in a group. This group may be the family, peer group, or work colleagues. Personal opinions are often considered less important than the group's opinion.

Obviously this can have negative implications for Bible study groups. Participants may be hesitant to share their own questions or their own response to the gospel. So it's important to foster an atmosphere that will help to overcome these reservations.

- Holding the Bible studies in someone's house is better than meeting in a coffee shop or public space.

- Sharing a meal together before the Bible study will help people relax.

- Be sensitive to the behaviour of those from other cultures. The apostle Paul adapted his behaviour in order to win as many as possible from different backgrounds: 'I have become all things to all men so that by all possible means I might save some. I do all this for the sake of the gospel, that I may share in its blessings' (1 Corinthians 9:22–23). This means watching, learning and following cultural cues. It might include addressing participants in a particular way; being careful not to point at people; if you share a meal, not eating with your left hand and so on. With a group made up of many cultures, however, it is impossible to be aware of, or to adapt your behaviour to *every* culture within the group. Don't spend time worrying about making cultural blunders. People will forgive you if they can see that you genuinely care about them.

- Group outings outside of your weekly meetings will help relationships to grow – for example, playing a sport or going to an appropriate movie.

- Don't lose touch afterwards. After the course has finished, whether or not participants have become Christians, try to stay in contact.

GROUP DISCUSSIONS

The idea of 'group discussions' might be strange to some participants. In many Asian cultures, for example, the 'teacher' is expected to impart information, while the 'student' passively absorbs.

In some cultures it is considered a virtue to remain silent, rather than bother the teacher or hold up the group.

- Explain that the group will learn together from the Bible.

- Make it clear to participants that they are free to ask questions whenever they want.

- Guide the group discussion and teach the gospel, but do not lecture.

LANGUAGE BARRIERS

If participants are struggling to speak English, they may feel embarrassed and therefore be reluctant to contribute to the discussion.

Sometimes, when participants come from the same country, they may fear 'losing face' or being embarrassed in front of their friends if they don't understand.

Moreover, studying the Bible will probably introduce new words to the participants.

However, for many, the attraction of studying Mark's Gospel in English will outweigh the language struggles they may experience. Also, Bible translations in most languages are available on the internet (visit BibleGateway at www.gospelcom.net) and can be used side-by-side with an English translation.

- As you prepare the Bible study at home, anticipate which words might be new to people. Be prepared to explain them simply and clearly.

- In the *Study Guide*, after a passage is read, the first question is always, 'Are there any words you do not understand?' Initially participants might be shy to admit this, so you may want to suggest the words you noted in your preparation.

- Be creative in your presentation. Use pictures, diagrams and illustrations to explain difficult words.

- Bear in mind that words and phrases familiar to Christians (for example, 'pagan', 'washed in the blood', 'house group', 'the Lord' and so on) may seem strange to those from other cultures.

EXPLAINING THE GOSPEL TO THOSE OF OTHER FAITHS

The Bible teaches that salvation is only possible through faith in Jesus Christ: 'I am the way and the truth and the life. No-one comes to the Father except through me' (John 14:6); 'Salvation is found in no-one else, for there is no other name under heaven given to men by which we must be saved' (Acts 4:12). While always being respectful towards people of other religions, we must hold firmly to the Bible's teaching on the uniqueness of Christ.

- In Romans 10:17 the apostle Paul explains that '…faith comes from hearing the message, and the message is heard through the word of Christ'. That means that you do not need a thorough understanding of Islam or the Qur'an before you can share the gospel with a Muslim. Nor do you need to be familiar with folk religion before sharing the gospel with someone who practices it. Although it may be considerate to have some background knowledge of other religions, it is the clear presentation of the gospel message that leads to faith.

- Religions may share words like 'God', 'sin', 'eternal life' and so on, but the meanings of these words are often very different. For example, to a Muslim, God is impersonal and distant. He does not love people or desire a relationship with them. To a Buddhist, the prospect of eternal life is something to be avoided, not celebrated. To a Hindu, Jesus Christ can be one among many gods, rather than the unique revelation of the only God. When appropriate, explain what the Bible means by these terms.

Session 3

Before the Course

To help your course run smoothly you will need to consider the following before the course begins:

WHERE WILL YOU MEET?

Find somewhere 'neutral' and unthreatening to participants, somewhere you are unlikely to be interrupted – a home is ideal, or a classroom, or a quiet corner of a canteen.

Make sure it is somewhere that's easy to find.

Try to find somewhere where you can meet every week at the same time.

HOW OFTEN WILL YOU MEET?

It is best to meet regularly. Once a week is ideal.

HOW WILL YOU INVITE PEOPLE?

Organise a guest event like a sports afternoon, a Christmas carol service, a visit to the cinema, a campus mission, a picnic and so on. At the end of the event, there should be an invitation to join **Christianity Explored**.

It may be appropriate to invite people personally to the course. Tell them that there will be refreshments / a meal, a Bible study, a short discussion and plenty of opportunities to ask any questions they want.

When inviting people to guest events or to **Christianity Explored**, it is important to be honest about exactly what will happen.

Reassure people that no-one will be expected to pray, sing or do anything that makes them feel uncomfortable or embarrassed.

WHO WILL LEAD?

Leaders should be Christians who are able to teach, encourage discussion and care for participants. They should be able to teach the Bible faithfully and clearly and be able to deal with difficult questions on Mark's Gospel. Rather than simply telling people about God's love, leaders must be willing to demonstrate that love by devoting time and attention to those in their care.

If there is only one person on your course, ensure that his or her leader is the same sex.

In a mixed group, it is helpful to have a male and a female leader in order to deal with pastoral situations appropriately.

This course material assumes that the leader has a very good grasp of the English language.

The studies are based in Mark's Gospel. As a result participants will have questions that are not explicitly dealt with in the material. It is assumed that leaders will have enough general biblical knowledge to help participants with these questions.

HOW WILL YOU PREPARE?

A well-prepared **Christianity Explored** leader will be dedicated in two particular areas:

1. Dedicated to the Bible

The Bible is God's word. Whenever we open the Bible, God addresses us. In Hebrews 4:12 we read: 'For the word of God is living and active. Sharper than any double-edged sword, it penetrates even to dividing soul and spirit, joints and marrow; it judges the thoughts and attitudes of the heart.' Nothing else can do this.

Because we're convinced of the power of God's word, every participant should be given a Bible at the beginning of the course. As leaders, our focus should always be on opening the Bible with people.

Read Mark's Gospel and familiarise yourself with the *Study Guide* part of this book. You will feel much more confident to lead participants once you've prepared yourself for the Bible studies that make up **Christianity Explored**.

2. Dedicated to prayer

Paul encourages the Christians at Colosse to devote themselves to prayer – in particular to pray for him in his evangelism. In Colossians 4:2–3 we read: 'Devote yourselves to prayer, being watchful and thankful. And pray for us, too, that God may open a door for our message...' Before, during and after the course we must pray.

Pray that those invited will attend the course, that God will open their blind eyes, for the logistics of organising the course, and that God will equip you to lead faithfully.

Mobilise others to pray. Evangelism is a spiritual battle, so ask other Christians to pray for you and for your group. Report back to them regularly so that they can pray for specific needs and be encouraged by answered prayer.

Session 4

During the Course

PREPARING BEFORE PARTICIPANTS ARRIVE

Arrive in plenty of time so that you can pray with the other leaders. Pray for individual participants, that the Holy Spirit would open their blind eyes, and pray for protection from disruptions as you meet.

Everyone on the course – leaders and participants – will need a Bible. For the sake of clarity, it is important that everyone use the same version. (The version used throughout the course material is the New International Version.) Participants should be given a Bible at the start of the course, preferably one they can take away with them.

Make sure you have enough copies of the *Study Guide* so that everyone can have their own copy, and don't forget pens.

WELCOMING PARTICIPANTS

Remember their names. This makes people feel valued and respected.

Take the lead in introducing people to each other. Always introduce new participants.

SHARING A MEAL

Eating together as a group is an important part of each week. Try to avoid heavy theological discussions at this stage: the aim is to relax together, not to be spiritually intense.

Sharing a meal should last about half an hour. If it is impractical to prepare and serve a meal, provide light refreshments (coffee and biscuits, for example).

Sit where you can see everyone. That way, you can make eye contact with people, and it also ensures that they can see you too.

It's not a good idea for leaders to sit next to one another, as it can look intimidating.

After everyone has arrived and you've had time to relax and chat together over a meal, begin the Bible study time. As leader, your responsibility is more than just asking the Bible study questions. You should try to maintain a relaxed atmosphere and involve everyone in the discussion if possible. Don't forget how important the tone of your voice and your body language can be as you lead the discussion.

As you'll see from the *Study Guide* section of this book, each study follows the same pattern:

Summary of what has been learned so far

Marked with the symbol

This summary gradually builds each week until, in Week 8, there is a summary of the entire course.

Feedback from the Home Study

Marked with the symbol

This gives participants the chance to ask questions arising from the passage they've been asked to read at home. Since not everyone will have done his or her Home Study every week, it's important not to make anyone feel uncomfortable. If nobody has anything they'd like to discuss, move on.

Opening discussion question(s)

Marked with the symbol

These questions are designed to open up discussion. Don't spend too long over these questions.

Read aloud from Mark

Marked with the symbol

It is a good idea to involve the participants by dividing the passage between them and asking them to read a few verses each aloud. Be aware of anyone who might not be comfortable doing this – especially in the first couple of weeks.

Questions on Mark

These always appear in grey boxes.

It is important to listen carefully to the answers given by participants and to reply graciously. Participants need to know that they are valued and that their opinions are important to you.

Encourage participants to write down the answers in the space provided in their *Study Guide*.

The answers are provided for you.

ADDITIONAL NOTES FOR LEADERS are included to help you prepare and are intended for your reference only.

Outline of what has been learned

Immediately after (and sometimes in between) the questions, there is a short outline of what has just been learned together with an appropriate picture. A leader should read this outline aloud.

Comments or questions

Marked with the symbol

This is a chance for participants to share their thoughts or ask questions.

Home Study

Marked with the symbol

Each week participants are asked to read a few chapters of Mark on their own at home and write down any questions they have. It may help to present them with a copy of Mark in their own language. Bible translations into most languages are freely available on the internet (visit BibleGateway at www.gospelcom.net).

Additional instructions for leaders

Marked with the symbol

These appear throughout the study and indicate an instruction for leaders that is not in the participant's guide.

ENDING THE BIBLE STUDY

Limit the study time to one hour. You should be able to complete the study in less than an hour, but if you are behind schedule, don't rush through the questions. Instead, complete as many as you can and finish the study at the start of your next meeting.

Always finish at the promised time. Good timekeeping develops trust in the group. People are then more likely to return.

Let participants know that they are welcome to stay and talk further if they like.

Time spent talking with participants after the study officially ends gives you a great opportunity to explore where individuals are in their understanding of the gospel. Seek to explain what they have not understood. Encourage them by sharing your own testimony if appropriate. Many people ignore the Christian faith because they feel it is not relevant to their experience of real life, so use this time to apply Christian thinking to their situation. Help them to see the need for a personal response to Jesus Christ, but do not pressurise them.

At the end of the course, it's very helpful to find out what you're doing right, and perhaps ways in which you might improve future courses. Give out feedback forms to participants at the end of Week 8. Not only will they be helpful to you, but they will also help everyone involved with the course to reflect on their own progress. A sample feedback form is below:

You do not have to answer all the questions if you do not want to, but please be as honest as you can.
Your details (optional):
Name _____ Date _____
Address _____
Telephone _____ E-mail _____

1 Before you began *Christianity Explored*, how would you have described yourself?
☐ I did not believe in God
☐ I was not sure if God existed or not
☐ I believed in God but not in Jesus Christ
☐ A Christian (that is, personally committed to Jesus Christ)
☐ Something else _____

2 Which of the following best describes you now?
☐ I understand who Jesus is, why he came and what it means to follow him. I have put my trust in him.
☐ I am interested in learning more but, as yet, I have not put my trust in Jesus
☐ Other _____

3 If you have not yet put your trust in Jesus, what is stopping you?

4 Do you know for certain that you have eternal life?
☐ Yes   ☐ No

5 If you were to die tonight and God asked, 'Why should I let you into heaven?' What would you say?

6 What would you like to do now?
☐ I am interested in joining a follow-up course (a course that will help me to continue in the Christian life).
☐ I would like to come to *Christianity Explored* again.
☐ I do not wish to do anything further.
☐ I would like to join a church.
☐ I am happy at the church I go to, which is _____

7 Do you have any comments about the course, either positive or negative?

Session 5

What Do I Do If...?

... THERE'S SILENCE?

If a question is met with silence, don't be too quick to speak. Allow people time to think. They might be translating the question, or considering how to phrase their answer.

If you sense that someone knows the answer but is shy about giving it, ask them by name. Often they will be happy to be asked.

If you think the question has not been understood, repeat it and, if necessary, rephrase it. (Don't ask, 'Did you understand the question?' No-one will answer that either!)

It might be appropriate to try a 'game' – asking them to raise their hand if they agree or disagree with certain answers as you give them.

It may help to divide people into groups of two or three at points during the study to work through questions and then have them feed their answers back to the whole group.

... ONE PERSON ANSWERS ALL THE QUESTIONS?

Thank them for their answers. Try asking the group, 'What do other people think?'

Direct a few questions at the other participants by name.

Sit beside the talkative participant the following week. That will make it harder for them to catch your eye and answer the questions.

If the situation continues, you may need to say something to the participant after the study and ask them to give others an opportunity to answer next time. (For example, 'Thank you so much for everything you are contributing. I wonder if you could help me with the quieter people in the group... ')

... SOMEONE GIVES THE WRONG ANSWER?

Do not immediately correct them. Give the person the opportunity to correct themselves. Ask them, for example, 'What does verse 4 tell us about that?' If they are still unable to answer correctly, give others the chance (for example, 'Does anyone disagree or want to add anything?').

If necessary, don't be afraid graciously to correct a wrong answer that may mislead others. Say something like, 'Thank you, that's an interesting point, but I'm not sure that's what's going on here.'

Have further questions in mind to develop the initial answer, for example, 'What did you mean by that?' or 'What does everyone else think?' or 'Where does it say that?' If no-one is able to answer the question, give the correct answer, showing from the Bible passage why it is the right answer.

... SOMEONE ASKS A QUESTION I CANNOT ANSWER?

Lead honestly. You won't be able to answer every question. Some questions can be easily addressed, but others will be difficult. If you don't know the answer, say so – but try to have an answer ready for the following week.

... PARTICIPANTS DON'T COME BACK?

Don't pursue them. In Mark chapter 4, Jesus taught us to expect negative as well as positive responses to the gospel.

However, if you've already established a good relationship with that person, contact him or her once to say you missed them, that it would be great to see them next week, but don't put pressure on them.

Session 6

Identity, Mission, Call

As a leader preparing to teach Mark, there's no substitute for reading through Mark's Gospel at least two or three times.

And as you read, you'll begin to see that Mark is preoccupied with three great themes:

* Who is Jesus? (Jesus' **identity**)

* Why did he come? (Jesus' **mission**)

* What does he demand? (Jesus' **call**)

Every passage in Mark has something to say to us about one or more of those themes.

Broadly speaking, the first half of Mark (1:1 – 8:29) is taken up with the question of Jesus' identity: it starts by saying, 'The beginning of the gospel about Jesus Christ, the Son of God' and ends with Peter's statement, 'You are the Christ.' The second half of Mark's Gospel is dominated by the cross, because Jesus' death is central to his mission.

By way of an example, look at one of the most significant passages in Mark's Gospel – Mark 8 verses 27 to 38 – and you'll discover all three themes in quick succession. Let's take a few verses at a time.

IDENTITY

The dominant question in verses 27–30 is Jesus' **identity**. Who exactly was Jesus?

'Jesus and his disciples went on to the villages around Caesarea Philippi. On the way he asked them, "Who do people say I am?" They replied, "Some say John the Baptist; others say Elijah; and still others, one of the prophets." "But what about you?" he asked. "Who do you say I am?" Peter answered, "You are the Christ." Jesus warned them not to tell anyone about him.'

People had lots of theories about Jesus' identity, just as they do now: 'Some say John the Baptist; others say Elijah; and still others, one of the prophets.' But Jesus gets very personal in verse 29: 'What about you?... Who do you say I am?'

Peter answers the question concerning Jesus' identity correctly: 'You are the Christ.' Jesus is not 'one of the prophets' as some were saying, he is actually the Christ: the fulfilment of all prophecy.

MISSION

But although Peter has Jesus' identity right, it's clear he hasn't yet understood Jesus' **mission**. Let's look at Mark 8:31–33.

'He then began to teach them that the Son of Man must suffer many things and be rejected by the elders, chief priests and teachers of the law, and that he must be killed and after three days rise again. He spoke plainly about this, and Peter took him aside and began to rebuke him. But when Jesus turned and looked at his disciples, he rebuked Peter. "Get behind me, Satan!" he said. "You do not have in mind the things of God, but the things of men." '

Here, for the first time, Jesus begins to teach them his mission – that he 'must suffer many things and be rejected by the elders, chief priests and teachers of the law, and that he must be killed and after three days rise again'.

Jesus doesn't leave any room for misunderstanding (he 'spoke plainly about this') because he knows that the disciples – and most of the public – have a very different expectation of what the Christ would be like. He would be a triumphant king, marching in to claim his territory, trampling the enemy underfoot and ushering in a glorious new era for his followers. A Christ who suffered and died would have seemed like a contradiction in terms.

Peter clearly has this triumphal view of the Christ in mind when he takes Jesus aside and begins 'to rebuke him'. But Jesus' strong reaction shows just how necessary death is to his mission: 'Get behind me, Satan!... You do not have in mind the things of God, but the things of men.'

The idea that the so-called 'Son of God' had to suffer and die is still a stumbling block for many people today. But if we're to understand Mark's Gospel – and indeed the whole Bible – correctly, it is essential to grasp the true nature of Jesus' mission: he 'must suffer' and 'he must be killed' so that we can be forgiven.

If that is what Jesus came to do, what are the implications for his followers? Let's look at Mark 8:34–38. What is Christ's **call**?

'Then he called the crowd to him along with his disciples and said: "If anyone would come after me, he must deny himself and take up his cross and follow me. For whoever wants to save his life will lose it, but whoever loses his life for me and for the gospel will save it. What good is it for a man to gain the whole world, yet forfeit his soul? Or what can a man give in exchange for his soul? If anyone is ashamed of me and my words in this adulterous and sinful generation, the Son of Man will be ashamed of him when he comes in his Father's glory with the holy angels." '

Having just spoken to the disciples about his own death, he calls the crowd to him and says, 'If anyone would come after me, he must deny himself and take up his cross and follow me.' It is striking, and not a little disturbing, to see Jesus immediately turn his attention from the cross he must take up, to the cross we must take up.

First, if we are to follow him, Jesus tells us we must deny ourselves. It is not a natural thing for human beings to turn away from their natural self-centredness and self-reliance, but that is Jesus' call. We cannot follow him unless we deny our own selfish instincts.

Second, we cannot follow Jesus if we are not prepared to take up our cross. We must be prepared to serve him – and others – to the point of giving up our lives. In effect, Jesus must be more important to us than life itself.

If that seems irrational, we need to hear what Jesus says next: 'For whoever wants to save his life will lose it, but whoever loses his life for me and for the gospel will save it. What good is it for a man to gain the whole world, yet forfeit his soul? Or what can a man give in exchange for his soul? If anyone is ashamed of me and my words in this adulterous and sinful generation, the Son of Man will be ashamed of him when he comes in his Father's glory with the holy angels.'

First of all, verse 35 gives a great reason to obey Christ's call: if we give up our life for him, we'll save it; and if we don't, we'll lose it. That's the amazing thing about Jesus – you give him your life, and you find it. People today are always talking about 'finding themselves'. Jesus is the answer to that quest.

Second, verse 36 says that even if we were to gain the whole world by rejecting Jesus, we would still lose the most important thing we have – our soul. That's a great reason for obeying Christ's call. What is the most important thing to us? Our college education, career, our boyfriend/girlfriend, family – or is it our soul?

The third reason to obey Jesus' call is in verse 37. If we miss out on eternal life, there is nothing we can do to buy it back. No wealth we may have accrued, no worldly wisdom, no friends in high places can win back the soul we have lost by not obeying Jesus' call.

And the fourth reason Jesus gives for obeying his call is in verse 38. If we reject Jesus, then he will reject us when he returns as judge of the world. So if the future belongs to Jesus, then it makes perfect sense to give him our lives, and our hearts, and our time, and our resources.

So that's Jesus' identity, mission and call in Mark 8.

You may find it useful to look through the whole of Mark's Gospel and decide what each paragraph has to say about Jesus' identity, mission or call. Label each one 'I', 'M', or 'C', remembering that some paragraphs may be a combination of two or three of the above.

Session 7

God's Role in Evangelism – and Ours

We need to distinguish between God's role in evangelism and our role. It's going to be incredibly frustrating if we try to perform God's role – because only the creator of the universe is able to do that.

Look at 2 Corinthians 4:1–6. 'Therefore, since through God's mercy we have this ministry, we do not lose heart. Rather, we have renounced secret and shameful ways; we do not use deception, nor do we distort the word of God. On the contrary, by setting forth the truth plainly we commend ourselves to every man's conscience in the sight of God. And even if our gospel is veiled, it is veiled to those who are perishing. The god of this age has blinded the minds of unbelievers, so that they cannot see the light of the gospel of the glory of Christ, who is the image of God. For we do not preach ourselves, but Jesus Christ as Lord, and ourselves as your servants for Jesus' sake. For God, who said, "Let light shine out of darkness," made his light shine in our hearts to give us the light of the knowledge of the glory of God in the face of Christ.'

GOD'S ROLE IN EVANGELISM

What is God's role in evangelism? God makes 'his light shine in our hearts to give us the light of the knowledge of the glory of God in the face of Christ' (verse 6).

In other words, God enables us to recognise that Jesus is God. God makes it possible – by his Holy Spirit – for a person to see who Jesus is.

The beginning of 2 Corinthians 4:6 reminds us that God said, 'Let light shine out of darkness.' That is a reference to the miracle of creation in Genesis 1:3. This same God who brought light into the world at creation now shines light into the hearts of human beings, enabling them to see that Jesus is God. In other words, for people to recognise that Jesus is God, God must perform a miracle.

People do not become Christians just because we share the gospel with them. God must shine his light in people's hearts so that they recognise and respond to the truth of the gospel.

And we know from these verses that people can't see the truth of the gospel because: 'The god of this age has blinded the minds of unbelievers' (verse 4).

Here, Paul reminds us that we are in the middle of a supernatural battlefield. The reason so many reject the gospel is that the devil is at work preventing people from recognizing who Jesus is.

The devil blinds people by making them chase after the things of this world, which are passing away, and which cannot save them. Their concerns are confined to the here and now: the career, the family, the mortgage, the relationship. They are blind to anything beyond that.

As a result, they can only see Jesus in the here and now, perhaps as a great moral teacher; his eternal significance is completely obscured. And, according to verse 4, Satan is determined to prevent people from seeing 'the light of the gospel of the glory of Christ, who is the image of God'. Satan does not want people to recognise who Jesus is.

OUR ROLE IN EVANGELISM

What is our role in evangelism? 'We… preach… Jesus Christ as Lord' (verse 5).

Our role is to tell people the gospel and leave the Spirit of God to convict them of its truth. The word 'preach' can evoke negative images, but it derives from a word simply meaning 'herald', someone who relates important announcements from the king to his kingdom.

Verse 5 also tells us the attitude we should adopt as we preach. We are to be like 'servants for Jesus' sake.' The word translated 'servants' literally means 'slaves' in Greek. Paul was determined to present Christ to others without any hint of self-promotion.

We must remember that the only difference between ourselves and an unbeliever is that God, in his mercy, has opened our blind eyes and illuminated our hearts by his Holy Spirit. We should be forever grateful, and so seek to promote Christ, not ourselves.

We must keep preaching Christ as Lord and, remembering that only a miracle from God can open blind eyes, we must keep praying that God will shine his light in the hearts of unbelievers.

2 Corinthians 4:1–6 also helps us to carry out our role in the right way: 'we do not use deception, nor do we distort the word of God... by setting forth the truth plainly we commend ourselves to every man's conscience in the sight of God... For we do not preach ourselves, but Jesus Christ as Lord' (verses 2, 5).

When we tell people about Christ, we should demonstrate the following qualities:

• Integrity – 'we do not use deception'. We are straight with people; we are genuine and sincere.

• Fidelity – we do not 'distort the word of God'. We have to tell people the tough bits. If – for example – we don't tell them about sin, about hell, and about the necessity of repentance, then we are distorting God's word. Preaching these hard truths means trusting in the work of the Holy Spirit to draw people to Christ, however 'difficult' the message.

• Intelligibility – we set forth 'the truth plainly'. We should always ask ourselves the question, 'Was that clear? Were people able to understand?'

• Humility – 'we do not preach ourselves, but Jesus Christ as Lord'. We must draw people to Jesus, not to ourselves.

As we use **Christianity Explored** to preach the gospel, we must remember that it is up to God whether somebody becomes a Christian or not. Only he can open blind eyes, so we must trust him for the results. God will do his part, and we must do ours.

CHRISTIANITY EXPLORED

SECTION 2
STUDY GUIDE

This section contains the studies to work through over the eight-week course. It contains all of the material in the participant's *Study Guide*, together with answers to each question and **ADDITIONAL NOTES FOR LEADERS**.

 Additional instructions for leaders are marked with this symbol.

Before We Begin

 The information below appears in the opening of the participant's Study Guide *and is printed here for your reference.*

Over the next eight weeks we will explore Christianity by seeing what the Bible has to say about Jesus Christ.

In particular, we will explore three questions about Jesus:

- who was he?

- why did he come?

- what does it mean to follow him?

The Bible contains 66 books. Many human authors wrote these books over 1500 years. God's Holy Spirit inspired each author. When we read the Bible, we are reading God's words – exactly what he wants us to know.

The Bible is divided into two main sections: the Old Testament and the New Testament. The Old Testament was written before Jesus was born and the New Testament was written after Jesus was born.

In this course we will read the book of Mark (also known as Mark's Gospel), which is a historical account of Jesus' life.

Mark's Gospel is divided up into chapters and each chapter is divided into individual verses, all of which are numbered. So 'Mark 1:1 – 3:6' refers to the book of Mark, chapter 1, verse 1, through to chapter 3, verse 6. All the Bible references in this *Study Guide* are written in this way.

During the course we will study various passages from Mark's Gospel. You may also ask any questions about Christianity.

So who was Jesus? Why did he come? And what does it mean to follow him?

Week 1

What is Christianity?

 Welcome the participants and introduce yourself. Please give each participant a Bible and a copy of the Study Guide. *Ask participants to turn to Week 1 on page 9 of their* Study Guide. *Briefly talk through the format of each week and then use the questions below to open up discussion.*

 What is your name? Why did you decide to come on the course?

 You might want to write down the participants' answers so you can refer to them later.

If you could ask God one question, and you knew it would be answered, what would it be?

 You might want to write down the participants' answers so you can refer to them later. You might also want to fill in your own answer and share it with the group.

 What do people usually think Christianity is about?

☐ Christianity is about being a good person

☐ Christianity is about going to church

☐ Christianity is a Western religion

☐ Christianity is about following the teachings of Jesus Christ

☐ Christianity is _____

Show participants where to find Mark in their Bibles and explain how chapters and verses work. Ask participants to turn to Mark 1:1. A leader should read the passage aloud and then the group should work through the questions below. The answers are printed here for your reference.

---

1   What do we learn about Christianity from this verse? (Note that the word 'gospel' means 'good news'.)

It is good news about Jesus Christ, the Son of God.

You might want to explain that 'Christ' isn't Jesus' second name, but the title given to God's chosen King and deliverer.

ADDITIONAL NOTE FOR LEADERS After his bold claim in the first verse, Mark quotes from Malachi 3:1 and Isaiah 40:3 which, in their contexts, promise a messenger who will announce the arrival of a rescuer King, the Christ, who will save God's people from judgement. The promise of a messenger is fulfilled by John the Baptist in Mark 1:4–8. His clothing (Mark 1:6) was like that of the Old Testament prophet Elijah (2 Kings 1:8). Mark is showing us that Jesus is the one the Old Testament was pointing to.

2   Some people criticise Christianity. They say:

> **'It is a list of rules.'**
> **'It is about going to church and pretending to be a good person.'**
> **'It is boring.'**

How does Mark answer these criticisms in Mark 1:1?

Christianity is none of these things. It is good news about a person, Jesus Christ.

Ask participants if they have any comments or questions. Use any additional time to deal with issues that may have arisen from the opening discussion questions.

 Each week participants are asked to explore a few chapters of Mark. Before next week ask them to read Mark 1:1 – 3:6. They have a section in which to write down any questions they'd like to discuss next time.

Week 2

Jesus – Who Was He?

 Christianity is good news about Jesus Christ...

 Ask participants to turn to Week 2 on page 13 of their Study Guide. Ask if anyone has any questions arising from the passage of Mark they read at home, and discuss as necessary.

 Introduce the week:

'I hope you can remember what we said last week. It was very simple, yet incredibly important. Christianity is all about Jesus Christ. That's why we began last week with Mark chapter 1, verse 1: "The beginning of the gospel about Jesus Christ, the Son of God." This week we will learn more about who Jesus was by looking at the evidence in Mark's Gospel. Mark gives us information so that we can build up an accurate, historical picture of who Jesus was.'

Now use the question below to open up discussion.

Who do people today think Jesus was?

☐ A good teacher

☐ A prophet

☐ A political leader

☐ God

☐ Other _____

 Ask participants to turn to Mark 2:1–12. A leader should read the passage aloud and then the group should work through the study below. The answers are printed here for your reference.

---

1   Are there any words you do not understand?

2   What problem did the four men have? (see verses 2–4)

They could not bring their paralysed friend to Jesus because there were so many people.

3   How did the men solve this problem? (see verse 4)

They made a hole in the roof and lowered their friend down to Jesus.

---

4   What did the men expect Jesus to do for the paralytic?

They expected Jesus to heal him. Note that Jesus had become well known in Capernaum for, among other things, healing the sick (Mark 1:21–34).

5   What did Jesus do? (see verse 5) Why do you think he did that?

Jesus said to the man: 'Son, your sins are forgiven'.

Jesus thinks the man's greatest need is to have his sins forgiven, not to be healed. This is because – as we will learn next week – sin is more deadly than any physical disability.

ADDITIONAL NOTE FOR LEADERS   Jesus is not implying that there is a direct correlation between the man's sin and his disability (see what Jesus says about the tower in Siloam in Luke 13:1–5).

6   Why were the religious teachers so angry? (see verses 6–7)

Jesus was claiming to do that which only God can do (forgive sins), something the teachers of the law saw clearly. Sin offends God. So only God has the right to forgive it. So they concluded that he was blaspheming.

7   What is the answer to Jesus' question in verse 9?

It is easier to say, 'Your sins are forgiven,' because that is something unseen that cannot be disproved. It is more difficult to say, 'Get up, take your mat and walk', because you can tell whether it is true or not.

8 Why did Jesus heal the man? (see verses 10–12)

Jesus healed the man to show that he has authority to forgive sin – not just the man's sin, but our sin as well.

9 In Mark 2:10 Jesus calls himself the 'Son of Man'. The prophet Daniel described the son of man 500 years before Mark:

'In my vision at night I looked, and there before me was one like a son of man, coming with the clouds of heaven... He was given authority, glory and sovereign power; all peoples, nations and men of every language worshipped him.' (Daniel 7:13–14)

In your own words, how did Daniel describe the son of man?

Jesus frequently refers to himself as the 'Son of Man'. It recalls Daniel 7:9–14, in which the 'son of man' was the name of the one who approached God (the Ancient of Days), and was given authority to rule over everyone forever.

You may need to explain that the quote is from the Old Testament and that a prophet was a man who spoke words that came from God. The prophets addressed their words to the people of that time, but often they also referred to a future event. Daniel's vision pointed to a future event.

10 What did Jesus expect people to understand when he called himself the 'Son of Man' in Mark 2:10?

He expected them to understand that Daniel was writing about him – that he had been given authority by God to forgive sin.

11 What does this event in Mark tell us about who Jesus is?

Jesus is God. By healing the paralytic, and thus proving that he has authority to forgive sin, Jesus shows that he is God. After all, 'Who can forgive sins but God alone?' (verse 7).

12 Who do you think Jesus is?

This question is designed to help participants apply what they have learned.

 The following outline also appears in the participant's Study Guide. *Please read it aloud.*

Jesus has power and authority to forgive sin.

Mark also shows that Jesus has power and authority:

- to teach (see for example Mark 1:21–22)

- over evil spirits (see for example Mark 1:23–27)

- over sickness (see for example Mark 1:29–34)

- over nature (see for example Mark 4:35–41)

- and even over death (see for example Mark 5:35–42)

The evidence in Mark's Gospel suggests that Jesus was a man with the power and authority of God himself. He is, as Mark says in Mark 1:1, the Son of God.

Ask participants if they have any comments or questions.

 Before next week ask participants to read Mark 3:7 – 5:43. They have a section in which to write down any questions they'd like to discuss next time.

Jesus – Why Did He Come?

 Christianity is good news about Jesus Christ, the Son of God...

 Ask participants to turn to Week 3 on page 19 of their Study Guide. Ask if anyone has any questions arising from the passage of Mark they read at home, and discuss as necessary.

 Introduce the week:

'Last week we asked, "Who was Jesus?" Whatever answer we give, it has to take into account the evidence in Mark. This evidence suggests that Jesus has power and authority over all things. This week we will ask another important question, "Why did Jesus come?" '

Now use the questions below to open up discussion.

What do you think is the world's greatest problem?

- ☐ War

- ☐ Poverty

- ☐ Pollution

- ☐ Racism

- ☐ Greed

- ☐ Other _____

 In last week's study, what was the paralytic's greatest problem?

 Ask participants to turn to Mark 12:28–30. A leader (or some of the participants) should read the passage aloud and then the group should work through the study below. The answers are printed here for your reference.

1   Are there any words you do not understand?

You may need to explain the context of the passage: 'Jesus was debating with the religious teachers when one of them asked him which was the most important of God's commandments.'

2   How should we treat God?

We should love the Lord our God with all our heart and with all our soul and with all our mind and with all our strength.

Since God made us and gives us every good thing we enjoy, and since he has power and authority over our lives, how should we respond to him? Jesus tells us: our response should be to love him.

And the really challenging word here is 'all' – love God with *all* your heart, soul, mind and strength. So no part of our lives should be withheld from God. He is to have all of everything.

3   How do we treat God?

We do not love God with *all* our heart, *all* our soul, *all* our mind and *all* our strength.

We decide exactly what we will do with our heart, soul, mind and strength. We give our hearts to lots of things, but not to our Creator. And instead of *loving* God, we live as if we *were* God.

None of us have loved God as we should. Instead of loving God, we have all turned away from him. We have all rebelled against God. This is called sin.

You may wish to use the illustration of family relationships:

'Parents are usually very kind and generous to their children, making big sacrifices for them – for example, in providing a good education. Some parents make financial sacrifices so that their children can study abroad. It would be a terrible and shameful thing for children to take all these gifts but then cut themselves off from their parents, refusing even to speak to them.

'This is how we have all behaved towards God. We are happy to take the gifts that he gives us – life, health, family, friends and so on. But we refuse to acknowledge that it is God who has given the gifts, and ignore him completely. This is called sin.'

 Ask participants to turn to Mark 7:20–23. A leader (or some of the participants) should read the passage aloud and then the group should work through the study below. The answers are printed here for your reference.

---

4   Are there any words you do not understand?

You may need to explain the context of the passage: 'The issue in this passage is what makes someone unclean in God's eyes. That is, what makes someone unacceptable to God. The Pharisees blamed external things – you are unacceptable because of what you touch, where you go, what you eat. The Pharisees and other religious teachers had many man-made religious traditions, which they thought made them acceptable to God. They accused Jesus' disciples of being "unclean" because they did not follow these traditions. Jesus replies to this and shows what real uncleanness is.'

ADDITIONAL NOTE FOR LEADERS Pharisees – This group did not just obey the Old Testament Scriptures but adhered to a stricter tradition, so they were seen as some of the most holy men in Israel. They viewed anyone who did not observe the same rigorous rules as a 'sinner' and an outcast (see Mark 2:15–16). Jesus called them 'hypocrites', which literally means 'play-actors', because of their public displays of religion and self-righteousness. He strongly condemns them in passages such as Mark 7:6–9 and Matthew 23.

5 Where is our sin?

Sin is within, in our hearts. Out of our hearts come the evils listed in verses 21–22.

6 What is the result of our sin?

It makes us 'unclean' before God. Because God is holy and pure, our sin makes us 'unclean' (that is, unacceptable) to him.

The evils that come out of our hearts make us 'unclean' before God. God cannot ignore our sin because of his purity and justice. That is our greatest problem.

Ask participants to turn to Mark 9:43–48. A leader (or some of the participants) should read the passage aloud and then the group should work through the study below. The answers are printed here for your reference.

7 Are there any words you do not understand?

ADDITIONAL NOTE FOR LEADERS Mark 9:48 is a quotation from Isaiah 66:24. It is a picture of the eternal torment that awaits those who have rebelled against God.

8 How will God judge our sin?

Our sin condemns us to hell.

According to the Bible, sin is ignoring God in the world he has made. It's rebelling against him by living without reference to him. Sin is not just about doing bad things. It is not just lust or dishonouring our parents or whatever. We may not have committed adultery or murder, but we have all said, 'I will decide exactly how I live my life.'

Now why is ignoring God in his world so serious? It's because if I insist on my independence in a world that God has made, then that has consequences. The Bible clearly links sin with death – and not just death here, but eternal death.

ADDITIONAL NOTE FOR LEADERS Jesus did not intend that a person should physically cut off a hand or foot, or pluck out an eye. Jesus is making the point that if anything is stopping us from entering the kingdom of God, it is better to take drastic action to rid ourselves of it, whatever it is, than end up in hell for ever. But remember that according to Jesus our problem is not our hands, or feet or eyes – but our hearts (Mark 7:20–23). We cannot cut out our hearts, so we are powerless to help ourselves. We need the rescue that only Jesus can provide.

9   Why is Jesus' warning so severe? (see verses 43 and 48)

Because hell is a terrible place of eternal punishment.

The reason Jesus warns us about hell is because he loves us and does not want us to go there.

10   What would you say if someone said to you, 'When I die God will be pleased with me because I am a good person'?

There is no such thing as a 'good person'. Nobody has loved God with all their heart. No-one has lived with him at the centre of his or her life. A person may be moral but still live in rebellion against Jesus Christ. It is this rebellion (which the Bible calls sin) that angers God. The punishment for it is hell.

 The following outline also appears in the participant's Study Guide. *Please read it aloud.*

We have all rebelled against God.
We all face his judgement.
We all need to be rescued.

That is why Jesus came.

Jesus said, 'It is not the healthy who need a doctor, but the sick. I have not come to call the righteous, but sinners' (Mark 2:17).

Jesus came to rescue us from the judgement our sin deserves. Next week we will learn how he does that.

Ask participants if they have any comments or questions.

 Before next week ask participants to read Mark 6:1 – 7:37. They have a section in which to write down any questions they'd like to discuss next time.

Jesus – His Death

 Christianity is good news about Jesus Christ, the Son of God. Jesus came to rescue us from sin, judgement and hell…

 Ask participants to turn to Week 4 on page 25 of their Study Guide. *Ask if anyone has any questions arising from the passage of Mark they read at home, and discuss as necessary.*

 Introduce the week:

'Last week we learned that we have all rebelled against God. We all deserve to be punished. We all need to be rescued. This week we will learn how Jesus rescues us.'

Now use the questions below to open up discussion.

Where do you see crosses today?

In Jesus' day, men were punished by being nailed to a wooden cross and left to die. It was a terrible and shameful thing to die in this way. God spoke about this kind of punishment hundreds of years before when he said, '…anyone who is hung on a tree is under God's curse' (Deuteronomy 21:23).

 Jesus predicts his own death three times. Read aloud:

Mark 8:31   Mark 9:30–31   Mark 10:32–34

What does Jesus say 'must' and 'will' happen? (Remember that 'Son of Man' is Jesus' way of referring to himself.)

 Ask participants to turn to Mark 15:33–39. A leader (or some of the participants) should read the passage aloud and then the group should work through the study below. The answers are printed here for your reference.

---

1   Are there any words you do not understand?

Read Mark 15:33 aloud again.

2 What unusual event occurred at mid-day (the sixth hour) as Jesus was dying?

Mark is counting hours according to the Jewish system, so the sixth hour would have been noon. At the moment when the mid-day sun should have been at its brightest in the sky, a darkness fell over the whole land and remained until three in the afternoon.

It could not have been an eclipse, because Passover always fell on a full moon and a solar eclipse is impossible during a full moon.

During a full moon the moon is here:

Now, for an eclipse to occur, the moon would have to be here:

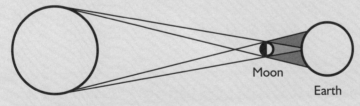

so that it can cast its shadow between the sun and the earth.

Moreover, solar eclipses never last more than about six minutes. This darkness lasted three hours.

So, something supernatural was happening.

3 **In the Bible, darkness is a sign of God's anger and judgement. What is surprising about the focus of God's anger?**

God's anger is focused on Jesus. But Jesus had led a sinless life. So it is surprising that Jesus should be the focus of God's anger and judgement.

ADDITIONAL NOTE FOR LEADERS See Amos 5:20; 8:9 and Exodus 10:21–23 for examples of darkness as a sign of God's anger in the Old Testament.

God's judgement fell on Jesus, instead of us.

 Read Mark 15:34 aloud again.

4 **What was the relationship between Jesus and his Father before the cross? (see Mark 1:9–11 and Mark 9:7)**

God the Father and God the Son had always enjoyed a perfect relationship of love. At Jesus' baptism and when he appeared in glory on the mountain, God the Father declared his love for his Son.

5 What happened between Jesus and his Father at the cross?

Jesus was forsaken by his Father. He cried out, 'My God, my God, why have you forsaken me?' On the cross Jesus was abandoned by God.

When Jesus died on the cross he carried our sin and suffered God's judgement on our behalf. God cannot tolerate sin so he turned away from his own Son.

God's judgement fell on Jesus because he was taking upon himself all the punishment that our sin deserves. Jesus died as our substitute, in our place, taking the punishment we deserve for our sin. Jesus paid the price for sin so that we never have to. He died for the sin of everyone who puts their trust in him.

You may wish to explain the idea of substitution:

'In many games of sport, one player will be taken off the pitch and another sent on in their place. This new player is the substitute. When Jesus died, he took our place in facing God's judgement for our sin. He is our substitute.'

Jesus was abandoned so that we do not have to be.

Read Mark 15:37–38 aloud again.

6   What happened in the temple in Jerusalem when Jesus died?

The curtain in the temple was torn in two from top to bottom.

7   The curtain in the middle of the temple prevented sinful people from entering God's presence in the Most Holy Place. It also protected the people from God's holiness. Only once a year, a priest was able to go through the curtain and enter God's presence in the Most Holy Place. But the priest could only enter after he made special sacrifices. How did Jesus' death change our relationship with God?

You might want to use this illustration: 'In some theatres during the interval a fire curtain will be drawn across the stage. This prevents access to the stage and, if there is a fire on stage, the curtain protects the audience from danger. Similarly, the temple curtain prevented access to the Most Holy Place.'

In Mark 15:37–39, Mark suddenly interrupts his narrative of the cross and takes us to the temple in Jerusalem. He does this to explain the result of Jesus' death for us. The curtain was like a big 'Do not enter' sign. It said loudly and clearly that it is impossible for sinful people like you and me to walk into God's presence. Then, suddenly, as Jesus died on the cross, God tore this curtain in two, from top to bottom. He did this to show that the way is now open for people to approach him. And that's only possible because Jesus has paid the price for our sin.

We can be accepted because Jesus died for us.
The way to God is now open.

---

8   **Isaiah prophesied about Jesus' death 700 years earlier:**

'He suffered the things we should have suffered. He took on himself the pain that should have been ours... But the servant was pierced because we had sinned. He was crushed because we had done what was evil... All of us are like sheep. We have wandered away from God. All of us have turned to our own way. And the Lord has placed on his servant the sins of all of us.' (Isaiah 53:4–6, NIrV)

Why did God's judgement fall on his servant Jesus?

This question is designed to help participants think about what they have learned.

9   **Will you let Jesus pay for your sin?**

This question is designed to help participants apply what they have learned.

The following outline also appears in the participant's Study Guide. Please read it aloud.

At the cross Jesus took on himself our sin and God's punishment for our sin.

Jesus paid the price for our sin so that we never have to.

As Jesus died, the curtain in the temple was torn in two from top to bottom. This illustrates the fact that Jesus' death opens the way for sinful people to come into God's presence.

Jesus' death rescues us from God's judgement.

To illustrate this, hold a blank videotape in your right hand.

'Imagine that this video is a record of your life. The Bible says: "Nothing in all creation is hidden from God's sight. Everything is uncovered and laid bare before the eyes of him to whom we must give account" (Hebrews 4:13). So everything that we have ever done, said and thought is on this video. There may be many great things on here. Perhaps there is a loving home, selfless acts, academic achievements, success in the arts or on the sports field.

'But there is also a lot on this video that you are ashamed of. Things you would rather people did not see. We all have secrets that we would hate to have people know about. But it is all recorded. And it records not just the way we have treated others, but the way we have treated God as well. The Bible's way of describing our shameful treatment of God and others is "sin".

'Now let's suppose that my left hand represents me,'

Hold out your left hand, palm uppermost.

'and the ceiling represents God. The Bible says that between us and God is our sin and it separates us from God.'

Place the video on the upturned palm of your left hand.

'My sin cuts me off from God; I am forsaken. But let me illustrate what happens at the cross.'

Hold out your right hand, palm uppermost. Your left hand should still have the video on it.

'Suppose that my right hand represents Jesus, and remember that the ceiling represents God. As Jesus hung on the cross there was no barrier between him and God. He always perfectly obeyed the will of God. But, while Jesus was on the cross, he took my sin.'

Now transfer the video from the left hand to the right, upturned, hand.

'That is why Jesus cried out, "My God, my God, why have you forsaken me?" as he hung on the cross. It could not have been his sin that separated him from God, because the Bible tells us that Jesus was free from sin. No, it was our sin that separated him from God. Jesus was taking upon himself all the punishment that our sin, everything on this video, deserves. Jesus died as my substitute, taking the punishment I deserve.'

Refer people back to your left hand, now empty, with your palm upturned.

'The result of Jesus' extraordinary self-sacrifice is simply this: we can be accepted by God. Jesus paid the price for sin so that we never have to. The amazing truth is that Jesus loved me enough to die for my sin and for the sin of everyone who puts their trust in him.'

Ask participants if they have any comments or questions.

Before next week ask participants to read Mark 8:1 – 9:32. They have a section in which to write down any questions they'd like to discuss next time.

What is Grace?

 Christianity is good news about Jesus Christ, the Son of God. Jesus came to rescue us from sin, judgement and hell by dying on a cross. He took the punishment we deserve…

 Ask participants to turn to Week 5 on page 33 of their Study Guide. Ask if anyone has any questions arising from the passage of Mark they read at home, and discuss as necessary.

 Introduce the week:

'Last week we learned that when Jesus died on the cross, he took God's punishment for our sin. As a result we can be forgiven by God. This week we are going to look at that a little more by exploring what grace means.'

Now use the question below to open up discussion.

If you died today, why should God let you into heaven?

God should let me into heaven because _____

_____

_____

_____

_____

 Do not ask participants to read their answers aloud. Instead use the following illustration. You will need to have each of the answers below written out in big letters on separate pieces of paper. Hold each of them up as you read them.

'Perhaps your answer is one that places confidence in what *you are*, or *what you have done*. Perhaps you wrote something like: God should let me into heaven because…

- I do not steal
- I do not lie
- I have never killed anyone
- I am a good person
- I go to church
- I do good things
- I have been baptized
- I pray *and* read the Bible

'They sound like good answers. But I can assure you that none of these things are of any use at all when it comes to entering heaven. There is nothing wrong with those things in themselves.

'It is good when people try to live honest, selfless lives. But the good things *we do* will not get us into heaven because they cannot solve the problem of our sin.

'In fact, *any* answer which places confidence in what *I am*, or *what I have done* is absolutely useless. Answers that begin "God should let me into heaven because *I*…" will do you no good at all.'

Gather all the pieces of paper with the wrong answers together and rip them up.

Ask participants to turn to Mark 10:17–22. A leader (or some of the participants) should read the passage aloud and then the group should work through the study below. The answers are printed here for your reference.

1   Are there any words you do not understand?

2   What did the rich man want to know? (see verse 17)

He wanted to know what he needed to do to inherit eternal life.

3   What commandments did the man say he had kept? (see verses 19–20)

The man claimed that he had kept the last six of the Ten Commandments that God gave to Israel (see Exodus 20:1–17 & Deuteronomy 5:6–21).

These are the commandments that described his relationships with other people.

The man should have noticed that the first four commandments are missing from the list Jesus gave him. Jesus is deliberately drawing his attention to these four commandments.

The first four commandments describe the way we should relate to God:

• have no other gods,

• have no idols,

• do not misuse God's name,

• keep his Sabbath.

Jesus' words show the man that, despite his claim, he has not kept the commandments.

Jesus wants him to understand that it's impossible for anyone to do so.

4   Read Mark 12:28–31. What did Jesus say was the most important commandment?

Jesus said the most important commandment is to love God with all your heart, soul, mind and strength. This summarises the first four of the Ten Commandments.

5 **How did Jesus show the rich man that he had not loved God as he should? (see Mark 10:21–22)**

Jesus told the man to sell everything he had and give his money away to the poor.

Jesus did this to show the man that he loved his money more than he loved God.

ADDITIONAL NOTE FOR LEADERS Jesus does not expect everyone to sell all their possessions and give their money away if they want to follow him, but he does expect us to love God more than anything else.

6 **The rich man loved his wealth more than he loved God. What other things do people love more than God?**

This question is designed to help participants apply what they have learned.

None of us deserve to enter heaven because none of us have loved God as we should.

Ask participants to turn to Mark 10:13–16. A leader (or some of the participants) should read the passage aloud and then the group should work through the study below. The answers are printed here for your reference.

7 Are there any words you do not understand?

8 What did the children need to do in order to belong to the kingdom of God? (see verse 14)

Nothing. The children simply trusted Jesus and came to him.

9 How can anyone enter the kingdom of God? (see verse 15)

Jesus is calling on the disciples to realise that they have nothing to offer and must therefore depend fully on God, just as a little child depends fully on its parents.

ADDITIONAL NOTE FOR LEADERS Jesus' phrase here does not imply innocence or purity – neither of which are traits of most children!

10 What was wrong with the man's question in verse 17?

The problem with the man's question is that he believes he can *do* something to inherit eternal life. He cannot, because – like all of us – he is sinful.

But, rather than treating us as we deserve, God in his amazing grace and generosity offers us forgiveness – forgiveness that is made possible by Jesus' death on the cross. We simply need to accept this gift from him. There's nothing we can do to earn it.

11 Ephesians 2:8 says, 'It is by grace you have been saved, through faith – and this not from yourselves, it is the gift of God – not by works, so that no-one can boast.' In your own words, what saves you?

This question is designed to help participants apply what they have learned.

 The following outline also appears in the participant's Study Guide. *Please read it aloud.*

We are all like the man in Mark 10. We do not love God with all our heart.

We deserve to be punished.

But God the Father loves us so much that he sent his Son to rescue us. He suffered the terrible judgement that our sins deserve.

We cannot earn God's forgiveness and eternal life by doing good things. God gives us the gift of forgiveness and eternal life if we simply put our trust in Jesus Christ. And that is grace: God behaving towards us in a way we do not deserve.

Ask participants if they have any comments or questions.

 Before next week ask participants to read Mark 9:33 – 11:25. They have a section in which to write down any questions they'd like to discuss next time.

Jesus – His Resurrection

 Christianity is good news about Jesus Christ, the Son of God. Jesus came to rescue us from sin, judgement and hell by dying on a cross. He took the punishment we deserve. It is only by God's grace that we can be saved…

 Ask participants to turn to Week 6 on page 39 of their Study Guide. Ask if anyone has any questions arising from the passage of Mark they read at home, and discuss as necessary.

Introduce the week:

'Last week we learned that there is nothing we can do to earn eternal life. We must simply receive God's gift of forgiveness through Jesus Christ. Jesus died to save us from our sin. But was death the end for Jesus?'

Now use the question below to open up discussion.

What do you think happens to us after we die?

 Ask participants to turn to Mark 15:42 – 16:8. A leader (or some of the participants) should read the passage aloud and then the group should work through the study below. The answers are printed here for your reference.

---

1   Are there any words you do not understand?

2   Why did the women go to Jesus' tomb? (see Mark 16:1)

They went to anoint Jesus' body with spices.

3   What were they thinking about as they went to the tomb? (verses 2–3)

They were wondering who would roll away the stone that was blocking the entrance to the tomb.

---

4   What did they find when they got to the tomb? (verses 4–6)

The stone had been rolled away.

Inside the tomb they saw a young man dressed in a white robe.

The tomb was empty. Jesus' body was not there.

The young man in the empty tomb tells them the reason why Jesus' body is not there. Verse 6: 'He has risen!' The tomb was empty because Jesus isn't dead anymore. He is alive.

5   The empty tomb should not have surprised the women. Why not? (see verse 7 and Mark 14:28)

Jesus had repeatedly told them that he would rise from the dead and they would see him again.

They've forgotten what Jesus told them would happen. Look at the young man's words in verse 7: '…go, tell his disciples and Peter, "He is going ahead of you into Galilee. There you will see him, *just as he told you*." ' This is exactly what Jesus said in Mark 14:28.

Jesus is always in control. He knows exactly how he will die, what will happen to him beyond death, and he explains everything to his followers before it happens. By now, the women should have learned to take Jesus at his word. And so should we.

6   According to the following verses, what did Jesus say he came to do?

Mark 8:31	Suffer, be rejected, die and rise again.
Mark 9:30–31	Die and rise again.
Mark 10:32–34	Die and rise again.

Week 6

7 Why did Jesus have to do these things? (see Mark 10:45)

Jesus came to serve us, to save us from our sin. He gave his life as the ransom price to pay God's penalty for our sins and set us free.

8 We have seen Jesus' power and authority over many things. What does his resurrection tell us about him?

The resurrection is further proof that Jesus is God's Son. No-one else has ever risen from the dead and remained alive. The resurrection conclusively demonstrates Jesus' power and authority over death – not just over his own, but also over ours. Jesus died and rose again, so also Christians die and rise again to be with God eternally.

9 How did the women react to Jesus' resurrection? (see Mark 16:8)

They were frightened and confused. They ran away from the empty tomb and were too afraid to talk to anyone about it.

10 What does this tell us about their understanding of Jesus and what he came to do?

The women did not have a clear understanding of Jesus' identity and mission. They did not trust what Jesus had told them. (See question 5, above.) They came to the tomb looking for 'Jesus the Nazarene' (verse 6) so they could anoint his dead body. They should have known that he was the Christ and would rise from the dead.

> **11** **Jesus said, 'I am the resurrection and the life. He who believes in me will live, even though he dies; and whoever lives and believes in me will never die' (John 11:25–26). What does Jesus' resurrection mean for us if we trust him?**
>
> We can be certain that our sins are forgiven and that we have eternal life.

 The following outline also appears in the participant's Study Guide. *Please read it aloud.*

God must punish our sin.

The punishment for sin is death and hell.

When Jesus died on the cross and rose from the dead, he took God's punishment for our sin and overcame death.

His resurrection offers great hope. It proves that there will be eternal life for those who trust in what Jesus did at the cross.

However, the resurrection is also a warning. If we do not let Jesus pay for our sin, we will pay for it ourselves for ever in hell (Mark 9:47–48) when Jesus returns to earth to judge us (Mark 8:38).

Ask participants if they have any comments or questions.

 Before next week ask participants to read Mark 11:27 – 13:37. They have a section in which to write down any questions they'd like to discuss next time.

What is a Christian?

Christianity is good news about Jesus Christ, the Son of God. Jesus came to rescue us from sin, judgement and hell by dying on a cross. He took the punishment we deserve. It is only by God's grace that we can be saved. Jesus rose from the dead, so we know that those who trust in him will have eternal life...

Ask participants to turn to Week 7 on page 45 of their Study Guide. Ask if anyone has any questions arising from the passage of Mark they read at home, and discuss as necessary.

Introduce the week:

'Last week we learned that Jesus' resurrection offers great hope in the face of death. It also provides a great warning: there will be a judgement and the risen Jesus will be the judge. We have talked about who Jesus is and what he came to do. This week we will learn more about what it means for us to follow him.'

Now use the question below to open up discussion.

Week 7

What do you think when you hear the word 'Christian'?

 You might want to write down the participants' answers so you can refer to them later.

 Ask participants to turn to Mark 8:27–38. A leader (or some of the participants) should read the passage aloud and then the group should work through the study below. The answers are printed here for your reference.

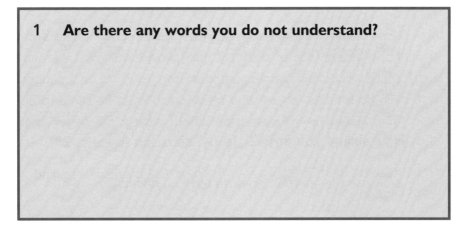

1   Are there any words you do not understand?

 **Who is Jesus?**

 Read Mark 8:27–29 aloud again.

---

2   What did Jesus ask his disciples in verse 27?

He asked them who people said he was.

3   According to verse 28, who did most people say Jesus was?

Some people said he was the famous prophet, John the Baptist, who Mark mentions in chapters 1 and 6. Others said he was Elijah, perhaps the best known and most influential prophet in Israel's history. Finally, others said he was perhaps another prophet. Everyone agreed that Jesus was a powerful speaker and a religious leader, but not many recognised his true identity.

4   Peter answered Jesus' question correctly. According to Mark 8:29 and Mark 1:1, who is Jesus?

He is the Christ and the Son of God.

5   How would you answer Jesus' question in verse 29?

This question is designed to reveal where the participants stand with Christ.

Week 7

What did Jesus come to do?

 Read Mark 8:31–33 aloud again.

6 **'Christ' is a title. It means, 'the Anointed One'. Anointing showed that God had chosen someone for a special purpose. 'Christ' describes Jesus' position and authority as the King who came to bring people into his kingdom.**

The people of Israel were expecting the Christ to come and save them from their enemies. What did Jesus say he had come to do? (see verse 31)

Jesus said he had come to suffer, to be rejected by Israel's religious leaders and be crucified. He promised that he would rise from the dead three days later.

7 **According to verse 32, how did Peter react to Jesus' teaching?**

Peter could not accept Jesus' teaching. He took Jesus aside and started to scold him.

8 **Why did Peter react like this? (see verse 33)**

He had in mind the things of men, not the things of God. Peter was thinking from a human perspective. He could not understand that the Christ would be Saviour and King by suffering and dying.

9 **God the Father's plan for his Son, Jesus Christ, was very different from Peter's idea. Think about what you have learned already. Why did Jesus have to be killed and rise again?**

Jesus had to suffer and die to save us from our greatest problem, God's judgement on our sin. He did not come to be served as a king, but to serve us by dying for us. He gave his life as the ransom to free us from our sin (Mark 10:45).

 **What does it mean to follow Jesus?**

 Read Mark 8:34–38 aloud again.

10 **What does Jesus demand of those who want to follow him? (see verse 34)**

First, if we are to follow him, Jesus tells us we must deny ourselves. It's not a natural thing for human beings to turn away from their self-centredness and self-reliance, but that is Jesus' call. We cannot follow him unless we deny our own selfish instincts.

Second, we cannot follow Jesus if we are not prepared to take up our cross. We must be prepared to serve him – and others – to the point of giving up our lives. In effect, *Jesus* must be more important to us than life itself.

Look at what happened immediately before Jesus says this. Jesus has been talking about his mission, about the cross. It's striking to see Jesus immediately turn his attention from the cross *he* must take up, to the cross *we* must take up.

It is costly to follow Jesus and will sometimes be painful for us.

Week 7

11   Why is it wise to follow Jesus, according to verses 35–38?

After presenting us with his call, Jesus gives us four reasons to obey it. With these four reasons he lifts our eyes from the present and fixes them on the future:

If we give up our life for him, we'll save it; and if we don't, we'll lose it (verse 35).

If by rejecting Jesus we gain the whole world, we still lose the most important thing we have (verse 36).

If we miss out on eternal life, there's nothing we can do to buy it back (verse 37).

If we reject Jesus, then he will reject us when he returns as judge of the world (verse 38).

12   In what ways would you have to deny yourself to follow Jesus?

This question is designed to reveal where the participants stand with Christ.

13   From what you have learned in Mark 8, describe what a Christian is. Use your own words.

This question is designed to help participants apply what they have learned.

14   Would you use the words above to describe yourself?

This question is designed to reveal where the participants stand with Christ.

The following outline also appears in the participant's Study Guide. *Please read it aloud.*

Who is Jesus?

Jesus is the Christ, the Son of God.

What did Jesus come to do?

Jesus came to die as a ransom for many. The only way sinful people can come back into a relationship with God is by Jesus dying in their place.

What does it mean to follow Jesus?

Jesus says, 'If anyone would come after me, he must deny himself and take up his cross and follow me.' Denying self means no longer living for ourselves but for Jesus. Taking up our cross means being prepared to follow him, whatever the cost.

Week 7

A Christian is a person who trusts and obeys Jesus.

Ask participants if they have any comments or questions.

 Before next week ask participants to read Mark 14:1 – 16:8. They have a section in which to write down any questions they'd like to discuss next time.

ADDITIONAL NOTE FOR LEADERS Most scholars agree that Mark's Gospel ends at chapter 16:8. The women flee still partially blind, like Peter, who had himself just denied Christ three times (Mark 14:66–72). The ending provokes the questions: Are you able to see who Jesus is, why he came, and what it means to follow him? (Verses 9–20 appear to be attempts by later writers to add a fuller resurrection ending to Mark. However, the oldest manuscripts do not include this section and its style and vocabulary are different from the rest of Mark.)

Week 8

What Next?

Christianity is good news about Jesus Christ, the Son of God. Jesus came to rescue us from sin, judgement and hell by dying on a cross. He took the punishment we deserve. It is only by God's grace that we can be saved. Jesus rose from the dead, so we know that those who trust in him will have eternal life. A Christian is a person who trusts and obeys Jesus.

Ask participants to turn to Week 8 on page 53 of their Study Guide. Ask if anyone has any questions arising from the passage of Mark they read at home, and discuss as necessary.

Introduce the week:

'Last week we learned what it means to be a Christian. Jesus tells us, "If anyone would come after me, he must deny himself and take up his cross and follow me." That means that being a Christian will not be easy. But Jesus also promises in another Gospel, the Gospel of John, that if we choose to follow him, God will send his Holy Spirit to help us: "I will ask the Father, and he will give you another Counsellor to be with you for ever…" (John 14:16). God the Holy Spirit will help you, guide you, comfort you, show you your sin and change you, enabling you to follow Jesus. With that in mind, let's look at our opening question.'

Week 8

Read again. Is there anything you do not understand?

Ask participants to turn to Mark 4:1–20. A leader (or some of the participants) should read the passage aloud and then the group should work through the study below. The answers are printed here for your reference.

---

1   **Jesus often taught people by telling parables. A parable is a story with a spiritual lesson. In verses 3–8 Jesus tells the story. In verses 13–20 he explains the lesson. Are there any words you do not understand?**

ADDITIONAL NOTE FOR LEADERS Parables are simple stories that teach deeper spiritual truths. Jesus explains them to those who listen (Mark 4:1–34). There is a spiritual principle here: 'whoever has will be given more' (Mark 4:25). The disciples were spiritually intrigued by the parables and drew nearer to Jesus to hear the explanation. However, to the unconcerned, the parables remained merely curious stories. They hear, but do not understand (Mark 4:12). The phrase 'otherwise they might turn and be forgiven' is a quote from Isaiah 6:9–10. From the context of that passage, it is clear that Israel had already shut her eyes and ears against God. Verses 9–10 in Isaiah 6 therefore describe God's judgement on stubborn hearts. The quote can equally be applied to some of those listening to the parables Jesus tells.

2   What does the 'seed' represent? (compare verse 3 with verse 14)

The word of God.

3   What happens when people hear God's word in verse 15?

Satan (another name for the devil) comes and takes the word away.

4   What happens when people hear God's word in verses 16–17?

People receive the word with joy but it has no root, so when trouble or persecution comes the hearer gives up.

5   What does it mean that a person who hears God's word 'has no root'? (verse 17)

Their response never goes beneath the surface; it remains shallow and superficial. As a result, peer pressure or opposition will cause them to give up.

6   What happens when people hear God's word in verses 18–19?

The 'worries of this life, the deceitfulness of wealth and the desires for other things' choke the word.

7 How do worries, money and other desires choke God's word?

If our time, energy and resources are focused on these things, they cannot be focused on God. We need to make a choice – as Jesus said, 'no-one can serve two masters' (Matthew 6:24). Worries, love of money and other desires are in direct conflict with God's word and, if we allow them to determine our choices, we will face dire consequences.

8 What happens when people hear God's word in verse 20?

People hear the word and accept it, and it produces a lasting effect.

9 Which of these responses do you most relate to?

This question is designed to reveal where the participants stand with Christ.

 Ask participants if they have any comments or questions.

The participant's Study Guide *contains the following explanation and 'prayer of commitment'. Please introduce it as follows:*

'As we finish the course, I want to say a few words about how we apply what we have learned from Mark:

Jesus is clear about the right way to respond to God's word. 'The time has come,' he said. 'The kingdom of God is near. Repent and believe the good news!' (Mark 1:15).

That means we must turn from what we know is wrong and trust in what Jesus has done for us on the cross.

You may still have questions. Or it may be that you understand who Jesus is, why he came, and what it means to follow him. You believe that Jesus is who he claims to be. You know you have rebelled against God and need him to rescue you. You want to accept God's forgiveness.

Here is a prayer that you can pray if you are ready to repent and believe.

I'll read the prayer aloud once, so that you know exactly what I'll be praying. Then, if you decide it's a prayer *you* want to pray, you can echo the words silently to yourself when I read it a second time. The prayer is also on page 58 in your *Study Guide*.'

Lord God, I have not loved you with all my heart, soul, mind and strength. I am sorry for the way I have lived. I have rebelled against you in so many ways. I now understand who Jesus is. I understand that when he died on the cross, he was taking the punishment in my place. He did this so that I could be forgiven and have eternal life. I gratefully accept that gracious gift. From now on, please give me the desire to obey you. Help me to live the Christian life, whatever the cost.

Read the prayer again. Read slowly, giving participants time to echo it silently for themselves. At the end of the prayer say:

'If you did pray that prayer, do let one of us know so that we can help you as you start the Christian life. I want to thank all of you for making time to come, and for contributing so much to the group. It's been a privilege to spend time with you.'

Please give participants the feedback form and ask them to fill it out. Give them a few minutes to do this.

*As this is the end of the course, expand upon the choices now available to participants (e.g. discipleship courses or future **Christianity Explored** courses). Since they have just read through one book of the Bible, you might want to suggest that they pick one of the remaining 65 and read through that. It may be useful to have Bible reading notes available to help participants who want to begin reading the Bible for themselves. Notes in many languages and in simple English are available online. You (and any other leaders) might also want to share with participants how and when you do your own personal study of the Bible.*

Further Exploration

 The information below appears in the participant's Study Guide *and is printed here for your reference. Please encourage them to look through it on their own at home.*

IF YOU ARE NOT A CHRISTIAN

Thank you for coming. Many people come to the course two or three times in order to help them understand Christianity. You may want to take the course again. Or you might want to meet with a Christian if you have other questions that you were unable to ask before.

IF YOU HAVE BECOME A CHRISTIAN

You are about to explore an amazing new life! Jesus promises that anyone who sincerely asks can be sure that their sins have been forgiven. It does not matter what you feel like. If you have put your trust in Jesus and are living to please him, you are now one of God's children.

When you become a Christian, God comes to live in you by his Holy Spirit (John 14:16–17). He is always with you. He will help you, guide you, comfort you, show you your sin and change you, enabling you to follow Jesus.

The next two pages will help you as you begin the Christian life:

As you begin the Christian life, we want to encourage you to do the following:

Read the Bible

God speaks to us through the Bible (2 Timothy 3:16–17). If you want to develop and maintain a relationship with God, you must make time to read the Bible each day.

Pray

When we read the Bible, God speaks to us. When we pray, we speak to God. You do not need to use special words. Prayer is simply speaking to God (Philippians 4:6–7). Although you can pray at any time, it is good to set aside a regular time each day.

Meet with other Christians

It is not easy being a Christian, so it is vital to meet with others who will encourage you (Hebrews 10:24–25). The best way to do this is to go to church. It is very important to find a church that teaches God's word faithfully, where the people support you, and where you are able to serve others. (Visit www.ifesworld.org if you want to meet with Christian students in your own country.)

There may be times when you doubt that you are really a Christian. You may wonder if God has really forgiven all your sins and loves you. You may ask yourself if being a Christian is really worth it. When you feel like that, remind yourself of:

Jesus' promise

Jesus said that he came to earth not to call good people, but to call sinners (Mark 2:17).

Jesus' death

When Jesus died, the temple curtain was torn from top to bottom. This shows that Jesus' death provides the way for us to have a relationship with God (Mark 15:38). Remember that you are saved not because of something you do. You are saved because of what Jesus has already done.

Jesus' resurrection

The result of sin is death. When Jesus died he paid the penalty for our sin. Death was not the end for Jesus. He rose from the dead and – because you have put your trust in him – you will have eternal life (Mark 16:6). As long as you trust in Jesus, you are sure of a wonderful eternity in heaven with him.

Acknowledgements

My heartfelt thanks go first of all to Stephen Nichols, Su Ann Woo, Sam Shammas and Barry Cooper who worked tirelessly to develop this edition of **Christianity Explored**. The long hours and loving care they have poured into this project have paid obvious dividends.

Alex Webb-Peploe drew the illustrations – some of them many times over – with patience, good humour and great skill.

The following people have repeatedly and generously donated their time and their talents to this project: Diane Bainbridge, Lindsay Brown, Lisa House, George and Rona Nichols, Tom Parsons, Andrew Rae, Stephanie Sim, Tara Smith, Paul Williams, Raymond and Doreen Woo, and many colleagues at Friends International.

Lastly to my brothers and sisters at All Souls Church, Langham Place – thank you for your prayers and unfailing partnership in the gospel.

Rico Tice
June 2004